T0279136

Shining Sheep

SEAGULL
BOOKS
•
CELEBRATING
40 YEARS

THE GERMAN LIST

ULRIKE ALMUT SANDIG

Shining Sheep

TRANSLATED BY KAREN LEEDER

LONDON NEW YORK CALCUTTA

This publication has been supported by a grant from the
Goethe-Institut India

  Landeshauptstadt
München

ARTIST
IN
RESIDENCE
MUNICH

VILLA WALDBERTA
EBENBÖCKHAUS

The translator was fortunate to be able to complete work
on this project during a residency in the Künstlerhaus Villa
Waldberta and the Lyrik Kabinett Munich, supported by
the Munich Artist in Residence scheme.

Seagull Books, 2023

Originally published as *Leuchtende Schafe* by Ulrike Almut Sandig
© Schöffling & Co., Frankfurt, 2022

Translation © Karen Leeder, 2023

ISBN   978 1 8030 9 252 2

British Cataloguing-in-Publication Data
A catalogue record for this book is available
from the British Library

Typeset and designed by Seagull Books, Calcutta, India
Printed and bound by WordsWorth India, New Delhi, India

Lumière!

in the beginning was shadow and shadow.

can you not hear it: this quiet?

the spirits tuning their instruments

just look about you: behind the audience

the film rolls are running. Lumière!

giving their all, the figures

on screen: warm machines.

in the beginning of the beginning was a dark

beginning, but balm for the eyes.

can you hear the bloodroar of bodies

in the half-light, in the auditorium?

keep turning metallic maiden

be godless and still. hey, what gods?

turn in a circle! Lumière!

only the instruments turn here.

shadow and shadow and—night!

without a voice no one can say

let there be . . .

ZIPPELONIKA

*ich kenne eine Frau
die hat Augen wie Kakao
eine dicke fette Leberwurst
das weiß ich ganz genau
und ich weiß auch, wo sie wohnt
nämlich dreimal hinterm Mond
und ich weiß auch, wie sie heißt
nämlich Zipp Zippelipp Zippelonika!*

—Anonym

*once there was a girl
with eyes as black as coal
a Leberwurst, nice and fat
yes, i know that girl
and i know where she lives these days
over the hills and far away
and i know her name and that's a fact
and it is Zipp Zippelipp Zippelonika!*

—Anonymous

o

last night
i was
woken up

because
suddenly and
what's more

without reason
i was
awake

Z

hello, today your Pixi is showing you
this picture puzzle: which of the two
pirate-girls will find the treasure

hello hello, today your Pixi is showing you
how to wrap up your pink lama
how to wake up your loser of a mama
how to tease her and spit on her
how to lay the kitchen table in her honour
how to lick your mouth clean and cleaner

hello hello, today your Pixi is showing you
how to make a nice dish of quark
that you can take with you to school.
to make this you will need
200 grammes of quark, black milk
and white liquorice made of sheep's wool
plus a little packet of sugar made from tears.

oh salty mama, go on, have a taste.

hello hello, today your Pixi is showing you
how to find your lanyard
how to not find the fags
how to strike a match
how to vanish in the shadow
how to take a 200-gramme stash
of silence and burn it into lama-coloured snow.

come and look, oh mama, it's snowing.

hello, today your Pixi is showing you
this picture puzzle: the way to school
has two times two right turns.
how many right arrows can you see?

I

the problem is

in every Zippelonika there is a Pixi.
but in every Pixi there's not a Zippelonika.

in every mother there is a daughter.
but in every daughter there's not a mother.

in every Zippelonika there is an Eliza,
a pike, a lip, a piano, a pain.

but in every Pixi there is only ever an x
and nothing else

P

last night
i was
woken up

because a
a part of my body
was hurting

a part that had
still not
grown.

jets
perhaps
or breasts

P

**on good days Zippelonika is a bouncy castle
with crenellations, a slide and flat blue insides**

and Pixi is nothing but a kid with big teeth
leaping against the soft walls at full tilt

on bad days Zippelonika is a fortress made
of foam, and Pixi leaps into emptiness

on good days Zippelonika is a rubber duck
bobbing on the surface of Pixi's yacking

on bad days Zippelonika is a zeppelin
as deserted as its own hangar

on good days Zippelonika is totally Zippelonika.
and Pixi is the one who once lived in her belly.

on bad days Zippelonika is stuffed full
of air like an out-of-tune accordion.

on good days Zippelonika is warm and light
and gently buffeted by Pixi's leaps of thought

on bad days Zippelonika is a jet plane
and Pixi a swarm of geese on collision course

but on good days Zippelonika is a bouncy castle
and not a machine nor foam nor stone.

E

last—ah—
last night
i was
woe
ken
up

because

L

once there was a girl,
would give her kid a hiding now and then.
she would hit her in the face and think to herself:
still, it's a good job that i never hit her little chest. that is
much worse than a clip round the ear. still, it's a good job
that i never hit her back, that can cause lasting harm
after all. i used to know a girl, with eyes as black as
coal, as she tipped her kid's milk into her
face. still, a good job it wasn't me.
that's not what goes on in good families.
it must have been a different
Zippelonika
who did
that

o

last night i was woken up because
everything was hurting. it was not

quite my cheek, my bum, my neck
that were in pain. rather my heart or

Pixi, my lama, or what on earth can
i call it, so that it will keep its

red trap shut. but **Pixi**, wide awake
asks me: so where does it hurt?

N

Chorale

so where did it hurt, when Zippelonika was a kid
so where did it hurt, when no one saw how she hid

so where did it hurt, when no one heard a thing
so where did it hurt, when they couldn't stand the din

so where did it hurt, when Zippelonika fell to the floor
so where did it hurt, when someone hit her some more

so where did it hurt, when Zippelonika went to cry out
so where did it hurt, when no one stopped to shout:

NEVER shall any calamity befall you, Zippelonika mine.

I

i was hanging onto a nice
fat Leberwurst
that
soared through the clouds
me underneath   holding on
with one arm   and who   i called up
to the clouds   will save me now?
the Leberwurst of course   could not
hear me at all   kept on flying further
and further   over the hills and far away!
at the start i remember thinking   look
at this place how exciting   insider tip.
but then after a while   i was like
hey how long's   this gonna last?
my arm is hurting   and anyway
why is everything   starting to sway
like my   tanked-up mama?
but just in that moment   i at last
found my lama   it was made
of stone-cold lava   drifting across
the moon-sea   like poppy-seed like kids
like crown caps   just before they sink.
i went to wave and   say hello and so
i let go like you do.   never has a Pixi
fallen more slowly   more slowly
to earth.   and ach
mama   i woke
up
even before
i burst out laughing

K

Drinking Song

i used to know a girl with eyes as black as coal
she had a fatty liver, oh yes, i knew that girl.
i know where she lives these days, over the hills and far away
and i know what she drinks, the kind of swill that stinks

and I know how she reeks of booze
in the morning on our way to school.
when she tucks me in her breath smells blue:
blue like bruises, blue like korn. my ma rules

on a dark-blue bouncy castle beyond the moon
and cries that no one tells you what it's like
to be a mum, says she'd sooner learn accordion
than be my ma. i used to know a girl with eyes

as black as coal. now drink your milk. not like that
or you'll get a slap, sings my Zipp Zippelipp Zippelonika.

A

Question

so	where does it hurt
where	does it so hurt
does	it turn without rage
it	turns a hurt page
hurt	wounded sonnets
where	rage sounds. the end.

SEVEN MARIAN SONGS WITH A HYENA

after a Madonna from Salzburg
made of painted lime wood, hollowed out at the back,
c. 1420

VII

the hyena is—almost—the queen of animals
say all those who celebrate her in song.

i sing of the hard above and
below of humankind and its

tiny bright clumps of darkness
and how little of it can be seen

from here, from this **Kapuzinerberg**
where there's—almost—no bittercress

to be seen, at least by me, who has no head
for botany and how it is above all this.

i sing of the hyena that dwells
in all masters, but i can't see much

of that either. only the up and down
of her bristly coat as she moves around

inside me: i have the measure of that.

VI

people think her cunning
but they entrust their secrets to me

like that Madonna from Salzburg, who
hasn't been able speak to God since

Saturday, only to Sister Elisabeth
with her black-rimmed nails.

her hands remind me **of Hélène**
whom i haven't wanted to see in years

though we have unfinished business

how i wish i could touch her breasts
she hides prayers in them

for the day that doubt might
have dissipated like a tumour.

V

they say a hyena has muscles
running along the side of her clitoris

that are longer, in purely anatomical
terms, than a **song for two voices**.

from the chorus of our little wall
we two, Holy Mary and me,

clearly see our humankind
in all its eager activity

but is that something you want to know

and how are we to tell them apart:
hearing, Hélène, and understanding?

IV

give me your crown, Mary, before
it slips off. for like the world it does

not fit **over your little face**.
for hyenas, they say, unwilling

penetration is impossible. a little
tuck under the spot on the coat

of the belly, just a little shift
of the angle, and no one can

fuck, says Mary, and inclines her head

III

by the by, how to sing of such small breasts?

is humankind the beast with the greatest
tendency to unrealized comparison?

i have to go soon, we both say
in the same moment

and close our red-rimmed **maws**
for an unspoken wish.

II

look here! i'm singing that wish after all
and that means it won't come true for me:

i wished i was the hyena in your
weak-hearted body. how i'd always dwell

in you. in all masters there dwells another beast.

I

do you see, already
another **echo** of these

songs with hyena

THE SILENT SONGS OF THE WALLS

*of a chapel next to Tiefenau Castle,
which is completely invisible, as it was blown up in 1948,
overheard on a day in the 21st century with few visitors.*

I

i have the same number of words inside me
as all of you have words, the exact same number

but how many times can they be combined? you
keep finding words that no one sang before you.

your godhead made you after his own image
stark naked, blind—wild things that you are.

i am naked and blind too. my heart is of stone.
you flit in and out, grow larger, have

young and soon you grow smaller again, smaller
until you can no longer be seen in your forests

made of gold-leaf and stone. in sinus curves
of a perfectly uniform tone, you come and go

come and go through the centuries
every one of your words I have stored in my

walls. little gods of mine! have you made me
after your own image? in the symmetry of right

and left and a perfect third thing
that is simply invisible—or empty?

i have so many words inside me
as many as murder ballads. in my emptiness

how splendid the Silbermann sounds, when a local girl
fetches the giant key from the farm next door

and plays through the night, just for the rose garden
full of roses and lilac, roses, martens and goose feathers

i have so many pipes in me, so many clowns, i could
sound like a karaoke chapel in a club in downtown Kyoto!

listen to the silent registers behind the wooden curtain
listen with hands over your ears. they are playing the litanies

of right and wrong. here's an example of wrong:
do you see the castle before my entrance portal?

you don't? it stands neither to left nor right
like the plundered goods you find in homes hereabouts

for who would want to let the good dressers
explode? i am the castle chapel without a castle.

you martens—with eyes closed you stare
at the beautiful staircases made of air

III

i have so many words inside me
as many as three centuries of Our Father on a loop.

                          once a year the local women come to make
                     me beautiful. don't wash the mouths of your little ones

with soap. use it to wash your
own hands. my walls record your prayers

                     curses and rose-laughter down through the centuries.
                               once (that was today) i spoke to you

who need houses that you can lock
to call on your godhead, about whom you say

                     he is everywhere. and indeed he is everywhere.
                          once the stone marten came up to my attic

it sounded like the riders of the apocalypse in training
for the end of days. and when the summer had passed

                     the universe simply looked right through me
                     the roof was so leaky. and when the winter had passed

i had three small stone marten young in me
they were naked and blind, for your godhead

had made them in his own image

FIRE EARTH WATER LEAP

four variations for Wilhelm Lehmann,
the automatic speech software Bruce
and your voice

plus a rhapsody

I

Fire

You

Wilhelm
But so fragmented that what he wants to say is not comprehensible
Where do poems come from? Often from the impact . . . and the source that
emerges from it . . . often quite simply from something with the physical eye
. . . How can one . . . How can one . . .

Bruce
Just imagine you have been torn apart by a grenade, one would be able tell
by the label to whom all the parts flying about belonged

just imagine it was simply a game with words   *You*
in the gym class of a non-partisan God
with white football shorts and a full beard
and long, hairy toes in his trainers
and we were his school class of future murderers
and traitors, saviours, heroes, mothers, whingers
with perpetrator and victim indistinguishably
folded into one another and all of us barely that
first, little, almost memoryless, decade old.

the Milky Way only a pigment disorder
on His forehead, His third blind eye as
he warms us children—for the Lord is
within and without, is cause, effect
blessing and curse—as he warms
the stiff little limbs of us children. FIRE!
EARTH! WATER! STORM!, He bellows and
blows his black whistle so that the little
white ball leaps up into the invisible.

at FIRE! you must fling yourself flat on the
floor, wherever you are. just imagine you will
be torn apart by a grenade if you lift your head
too high. we throw ourselves flat on our stomachs
and close our eyes to know our enemy.
he lives in our own heads and looks just like
—everything you'd expect of—us. today
our enemy has left behind his sports kit with its   *Wilhelm*
sewn-in name tags, it wasn't you. just imagine   How can one ...
the whistle blows from above and you are torn apart   How can one ...
by a grenade. how should i know to whom the tattered
body parts belong, without sewn-in name tags.
                                                                    Wilhelm
                                            How can one reach the depths?

II

Earth

You

Bruce
The company swarmed onto the newly ploughed field.
Bright green stems of garlic still standing fresh in the meagre soil. Dig in!

eingraben. digging in.
night. then rain came
in sheaves, bright ring
bleeds. benign being
goes running ragged
into rocks again. so m-
uch anger here in being
near. itch back of fear.
B calls her N. black bitch.

beginning to get in g-
ear: be gone desire. this
garbage her inner rage?
her so engaged, bare,
in range. this here is
her grave. her left afr-
aid, the rage-binge near-
ing. gave all to save. B:
'nein?' this is all staged!

eingraben? ire began
in her, growing big:
not digging in fear, not

digging a grave. light-
child she heaves, sheer
she-bear, not birthing
a slave. she bore an N.
but N's dug in deep,
no guile, lost in sleep.

whether to weep? no!
she will begin again, grin,
grab Baeren-Gin, bear it
bear again, wear her scars
inside, stars by her side,
her heart on her sleeve.
was greed, and disdain,
inner pain: face forwards
now whatever remains. B:—

III

Water

You

Bruce

Nuch fanned out with his group, threw himself down behind a thistle;
the purple head was dusted with rain.

just imagine, He does it again, although
He promised He never would, and even
pinned a rainbow under the blue ceiling

of his gym so that you would believe
him. WATER, He cries and the little white
ball of the third eye on His forehead

starts moving, and you charge off towards
the wooden benches, standing in rows
in front of the wall-bars. anyone not at the top

on count of three, He yells, in his snow-white
gym teacher's kit, has lost! just imagine how
the rain is dripping completely and without

comprehension from the ceiling and—as time
stands still and you watch the rain crashing
watch the crashing itself—it runs down your cheeks

IV

Leap

You

Wilhelm
How can one reach the depths, before the surface is spread out
before our eyes? There is no last without the last but one.

Bruce
And everything depended on this leap: the earth, the heavens, the people.

there is no 'just imagine' without the 'just'.

there is no first without the second.

and everything depended on these people: the leap, the
earth, the heavens.

there is no gym teacher without the class.

there are no first ones without the last ones.

and everything depended on these heavens: the people,
the leap, the earth.

there are no perpetrators without the 'them'

there are no sacrifices without the 'i'.

and everything depended on this earth: the heavens, the
people, the leap.

there is no last without the last but one.

there is no 'there is no' without the 'there is'.

Wilhelm
So where do poems come from?

Fire   *You*

Rhaps

ody of L-

osing (after the

poem 'To My Son' by Wil-

helm Lehmann) the yellow blanket

on which i read poems about poems to you

the endless rapeseed in the almost

endless field behind the

house of my parents

my child, they

bloom a

t

par

rans

t

mitted

by a satellite that

is passing high above our

house and garden this moment

while we two are sitting on the outermost

branch of a fractal of carpet squares

and rapeseed, you: mummy

look, a beetle! make

it go away

see

now

my child

!

this beetle here

is without doubt an ant

looking for its way home. coolly

i blow it back into the green chaos while

you clamber on my back shouting: look out

there are beetles everywhere and

they're attacking us! but see

here, if anyone is

attacking

the

n

the
attackers
are always lying
on their blankets in summer
next to endless fields of rapeseed.
just so. what, child, are you afraid of?
but we are invincible, you shout
we're the biggest parasites!
you laugh like the sun
at your back and
and i say al   how
most   the years
            .   go racing by on
              yellow carpets leaving
          us behind. i hope i will still have
         time to teach you what losing is before
       i sit down on my own and start the search for
      home (see how i'm chasing on ahead).
     but know this: the attackers, they
      are always us. the attackers
it   never attack on their
is us   own ter-
the parasites   rain
on yellow blankets on
yellow blankets on yellow blan
if we don't make them go, then others
will attack, the ones we sell our weapons to.
please make them go away, will you
oh. blooming quadrature
one hundred blasted
years after
a lost
war

SHINING BODIES

Murmurations. Small Choral Piece with Braces

                              c c
                   c c
                   can
        you hear r r r r
       hear r r r r it
     it t t t t
     it t t t t what
                what t t t t
                what t t t t they murmur
                              they murmur the e e e e
                              they murmur the e e starlings
        can you hear what they murmur the starlings across the meadows
          with their outstretched feathers they write themselves
          into the open pages of the yearbook of spring
        see how they formulate (not): i am (not)
        you are (not) we all are
                   ((((never never ever ev ev
                              er er ever))))
                        alone a all
                        all all
                        one one
                                 n n

Guidance on Laughing at a Distance

first the bad news: everything that is everything to you will shrink to the size of an insect on the fastened window.

but it will do that even if you don't follow this guide.

now this is where the good news should come.

but do we know who will still be there after this guidance on laughing at a distance? the insect or Lynn's ex, or Lynn or her ancient, laughing parents?

and now for the good news: screw all the magnificent avenues and squares. we will meet each other in forests. all the oxygen will make us totally high.

and we will walk at a bit of a distance: hands loose at our sides, right foot back, left foot back. and so on.

it will be a whole new feeling to watch nature as it purrs on past and overtakes you.

in the bark of a tree we will scratch: Lynn was here.

in the bark of another tree we will read: come here = go away!

we will spell out the cheerfulness between the trees, and this is how it will be: bend down briefly. wash your hands in the leaves. sing Happy Birthday twice.

Happy Birthday to you, squashed tomatoes and stew. i've got your presents, and your cake too.

now the laughter should already be noticeable. most people feel a distinct tickle in the larynx. right here.

Happy Birthday, Lynn! we will shout and burst into laughter at the answer in the echo of the trees.

and there it is, like being high again. not because of all that oxygen around you, but because you can hardly catch your breath for laughter.

slowly, it starts to feel like you're trying to breathe through a straw. some deal with that better than others.

but more than anything, it's an infectious laugh that gradually spreads to all of us, until the whole forest is quivering in a single great laughter.

in the end you will be lying on the ground just laughing a little until you really can't any more.

the real challenge is not to stop laughing. humour is when you laugh anyway.

this can also be done lying down.

laughing, you'll look up at the outline of the laughing sun. dark and small, it hovers like a laughing insect over the canopy of the trees.

and that is both good news and bad.

Climate change is here, now. But we are also here, now. And if we don't act, who will?

Inger Andersen, Executive Director of the United Nations Environment Programme

just let that melt on your tongue:
shining sheep, genetically modified
as night storage for the dark hours

visible in satellite images as little ghosts
their delicate shimmer on the radar
seems to be made to lull

the oppressive darkness between
the great golden bulls of the cities
into a comforting gleam.

that we can do. dressage of a certain kind.
but we cannot get the dusty fossil taste
of coal out of our tongue

or maybe we can? what is the radiation
of the fuel elements under our trainers about?
that which is hidden cannot be seen from

the highest peak, unlike the wall of fire
that divides a country in two down the middle

like the little man with anger issues
when someone knows his true name
ˈlɔɪ̯çtn̩dəˈʃaːfə
loik-tender? shah? fer?

this audio example is man-made.

my sound cosmonaut, tell me
does silence really sound like
this deafening bleating?

on the wall in our hall hangs a picture of Inger Christensen
in front of a sky-blue Fibonacci sequence:
0
1
1
2
3
from her mouth
an atomic shining
that despite all better
judgement cannot stop

From the Water

comes all that speaks.
the water does not care
that everything we are
is made of water, as children
are made of their progenitors'
faulty gene-set that splits
into its component parts, like
the ghost of a fluid returning
to nothing but two gases. we will
wish one day we could
dissolve our own parasitic kind
into morning mist. but
take care what you wish for.
once we wished for one who
would come and turn water
into wine. it's all the same
to the water. we will wish
we could escape the levels
that keep rising year
on year, even if only
for one day a week:
a Friday, perhaps

Of Losing

grain of salt, grain of salt
please let
me laugh
but ach
this rage i've felt

this rage i've felt
that i laugh
please let
it pass
grain of salt, grain of salt

come to a halt

The tongue is a needle. And I am True North. Telling lies.

late underdogs rattle in the home, ingest all. 'Nu ein Ei'! hide it in a hat. Lea runs legend-lost to unreel teeming data. hello, in line! no using the ultra-green tides. meet a satellite retinue hounding neater gold helmets in to nature! genuine stellar lights, one alien theme. did someone tell a lie? Lea, treading dust, uttering her inner need to linger: slum it, atone, still aged heath, ennui. latent turn made true. the Gili-isles inhaled. gone. one nitrate hell intuited, almond Lea's egg-rite unseen. oh! the north ill, undone. see Lea, mud-genii, greet Atlantis. The tongue is a needle. And I am True North. Telling lies.

follow the instructions: take part.

be part of the noise. be an audible disturbance in the transmission field.

be the spinning of a ship below the satellite.

spread your arms out wide. be **Open Arms**. hold your own.

hold this position. hold out in this position.

use your hands. share fresh water, documents and comfort.

share the beach of your childhood holidays with open hands

share what runs away between your fingers. share what you don't have.

hold the jumper back from jumping. hold the hands of children.

gently take the child from its mother's lap. stow it away in the fridge.

hold your hand in front of your face for a moment. return to your position.

hold human rights before the law. hold out against the screaming of sirens.

take help from the helpless. listen to the drowned.

do not listen to the voice in your head that says: strike sail.

hold your ground here off Lampedusa. don't believe them.

don't accede to their demands.

head for a harbour. set your course.

Internal report of a Russian spy software on the up-to-the-minute state of its unsuspecting informant, codename: Cents (leaked)

Leipzig, Nikolaistraße, Motel One.

Cents, 30 years old, diamond merchant
with a Belgian passport and no known
religious confession, missed her
connecting flight home from
Moscow. observing a roaring fire
on the motel TV-screen and with
the laughter of her Catholic grandma
ringing in her ears, Cents suddenly, i.e.
out of nowhere, begins talking to herself:

an end of Belgium is not in sight?
no, this flamed beginning is out
of sight! i'm no unending table. is
Belgium not an end of insight? is
tennis gnomish, a guide to bling?
not Belgium! fashion its ending
of nonsense, minuting a blight, i'd
be it in M.—a good light. funniness?
(not): an end of Belgium is in sight.

what was all that about? Cents asks herself
the morning after. speaking in tongues or
all that vodka back on the plane?
on the motorway heading towards the terminal
the taxi driver says he has been to Holland

three times, Dutch women, he says
are the most beautiful. still in the plane
she decides to change tack from a life of
diamonds to professional hits, and plunges

through the cloud cover over Europe

saʊnd bɒdiz

In a forest dell there lies a house,
Ruined since the woodman's death,
There 'neath the vines and boughs,
I oft-times go to seek my rest.

—Annette von Droste-Hülshoff

come on   i'll build us a house
made of propane gas and flame   are you one of those
lousy fathers out to screw with my mind with that iron will of
yours, 'cos men are mechanics after all?

am i one of those miserable moms
playing dumb with their kids, leaking their feelings all over the shop? come on.

we lay in the waving grass turning over those damned silver leaves one by one. but
were always one short. is there enough to paint the walls? is there the stuff for us
to have it all: the house with silver forks a golden retriever?

you and me   we are
so done with these old family homes.

i am the kid with the aviator goggles and you
my Hans with breadcrumbs in his head.

man   i want more than to read the coffee
grounds of chromosomes and that in the past tense!   so you take
your retriever and me my norm   we'll leave nothing here.

oh
above the ruffled fur-formation of this golden summer land-
scape a balloon rises into the sea of air.

okay   let's say a
single pinch of pathos as ballast. no more on board!

in a forest dell there lies a house   ruined since
the woodman's death. there 'neath the vines
and boughs, i oft-times go to seek my rest.
fir-
cones above us, cornflowers, poppies
candles in all the trees   a party!

a balloon can sink   just think.
a balloon can't be steered. so
write it into the warmer air:

we were here.
you were propane
& i your flame.

bittersweet ode-zine 1 (N)

hey boy, go to sleep = wake up!
you can't make a meal of yesterday's
snow nor your sister's laughter
in the east of the city, though you
long for nothing more fervently than
the sight of that shining fridge light
beaming out wide in every direction
right? the Amazon depot in Leipzig
is sending its workers home
because Father Frost is shedding
a Ural avalanche of snow on the roof.
it is snowing, snowing and snowing
nothing else will happen here today.
so lights out, Tobi, tomorrow you
will order from Obi, no from Bofrost,
the coolest frozen multipacks, so you're
part of a movement at last and
not so alone. but later tonight when
your hypothalamus comes rat-a-tat-tat
and presses the hunger button just like that
proudly take your pick (JA) or (NEIN) but
take note of my nagging: firstly
before you can say Yes, you have to
learn to say No, and that
also beneath stars and snow.

bittersweet ode-zine 2 (J)

jetzt toben sie wieder
jitterz between Sowie-
t e-zone, West Jedi tribe.
i jet to be westernized.
West? jeez, i'd bet Orient.
we'd breeze it, jettison
jobs, twitterize—end ee
JIT, downsize. beret, tee:
bitter, Sido? Zen? wee jet-
joint: we'd better seize
Tibet? *njet*! we desire Oz
e-biz, not jets, we're tied.
best we doze, n' jitter: i.e.
jetzt toben sie wieder—
eejit debt: twin-zeroes.

Friedrich Hölderlin, reworked

As when on holidays, to walk out and see the field
he stood behind the house, so we stand here and there.

From a night of heat the cooling lightning fell
across this heath too, fairy lights, foreign fields.

And the stream returns once more between its banks
and i too fall back into bed in a single stroke.

And with the heavens' delighting rain
i still drip when i'm fast asleep again.

In quiet sunlight stands the grove of trees:
clearly audible, the drying of things in us.

Like this they stand in favourable weather
as we stand forgetting how things bleed away.

All-present with a light embrace
forgetfulness teaches us to be the idiots we are.

For when in certain seasons of the year nature seems to sleep,
she does not really sleep, but beats

The poets' faces also sorrow—go on now, blub!
her fist at our throat as one beats sheep at shearing time.

For even when she rests, she senses what will be.
as one rests when one forgets as soon as it is done.

But now the day breaks! Waiting, I saw it come
but now it makes me mad!

For she herself, who is older than the oldest sheep
older than the shearing, older even than the shearing-blade

Nature now has woken with the sound of arms
our light strings stretched across the night are all the same to her.

By established law, as in former times, born from holy Chaos
she shears patterns in logical series, cuts us off—in one go.

Creator of all things, once more—you ask where she is?
ask instead can you bear her, blow after blow?

say: shining sheep, **shining sheep**.
shining sheep, Friedrich. and now

go to
sleep.

Daniel dreaming

Daniel dreams of sleeping.
Daniel counts sheep
in his sleep.

sometimes that goes
on past midday.
Daniel! do you shiver

beneath the afternoon moon?
abstinence is power.
Daniel dreams

his dream
of the dream
of a

laughing
sheep.
stop

now.
but
Daniel

Daniel counts
calories. fuck, what's
that muck in my bowl?

Frusties.
Daniel, go on, just take a bite.
Daniel so thoughtful and fat.

Daniel is cleaning up his stomach
he dreams of horns
nation-building

rulers, power.
Daniel is making a start
with his own body.

Daniel is making a start.
Daniel counts 372 kcal
Daniel!

don't keep thinking about
the children in Somalia!
Daniel is thinking about

1 ram with
1 diadem made of
7 curved horns.

each night he loses
1 in the struggle.
what does he have left?

Daniel, the last unicorn
is the last to understand
its own dreams.

Daniel dreams of reduction
versions of versions
of Daniel himself

and the best is the one
where he is as absent
as light. Daniel!

count it up again
fuck. what about the milk?

Daniel takes a rest from himself.

Daniel shines in his sleep.
less food
= more

radiance.
Daniel so light and empty
and indestructible

Daniel dreams again
Daniel dreams like
Daniel

LAMENTATIONS IN VI ROUNDS

round I

the little man inside my head is Omid.
he makes his rounds through all the wonders
of my brain, running with the wariness
of the hunted, who are used to being hunted.

my wonders leave him cold. the little man
inside my head is always running, never
on his way. a number in his passport even
forbids him from shitting. he calls it his 'eftetherain . . .'

his 'leave to remain' beats as the phantom heart
in the throat of a runner who is used to pain.

round II

the little man has a wife, who sometimes
takes pills for the pain. the little man's wife lives
inside his head. women like her never escape
singly from the regions of the heart, its strange

chambers of wonders, he says. she measures his
pituitary ready for the ninth cot. she swallows
tablets for her weak heart and for the pear tree
in her head that rustles like the pear tree in the yard

once did at home. its leaves fill her up. she fills
Omid up. round and round he runs in my brain.

round III

the little man inside my head, he had
seven sons. the first was at the bus stop
when a drone attacked. the second blew
himself up. the third counted to a thousand

as the teacher's throat was cut. the fourth
stayed at the coast, took a job smuggling
his own people. the fifth fell out of the boat.
his youngest don't understand the little man's

words any longer, they play on my aorta, Omid.
they laugh in their sleep. the only ones left to you.

round IV

the little man inside my head, he had
a daughter. he loved the way she boiled
minced beef, the way she answered back.
he loved the wonder of her eftetherain in Omid.

Omid sold his daughter in exchange for the value
of a ticket to Germany. today she called him up.
she sounded like she was sitting in his ear.
the pear tree in the yard was doing fine.

she hadn't been outside for weeks, she said. oh outside
says Omid to himself, there's nothing for you there.

round V

the little man inside my head, he had
a brother. he used to help the Germans
finding words in his land and for that
he lost his life. you haven't lost it yet

هرورو, Omid types into his phone and adds
a brother heart. you've made it to the safe house
you know what that means! but his brother knows
how to translate 'lip service' into Pashto.

off to the airport now, is the last thing that he
writes. back in touch when i know i'm safe.

round VI

the little man inside my head reads Ovid.
he reads him in the leaves of the pear tree
in his wife's head. she understands the words here
better than him, but cannot write a single one.

Omid reads Ovid in his daughter's Skype.
since her marriage she cannot keep her hand
from shaking. this Latin is all Greek to me, he says.
she shouts into her phone: بابه جان i can't hear you!

eftetherain comes the sun! Omid's wife cries out in pain
with the singsong of those who are used to labour pain.

THE SONGS OF THE RADIO TOWER

after Walter Ruttmann's film
Berlin: Symphony of a Metropolis, *1927*

ACT I

Min 0:00 Film starts

Shadow and shadow and—night!
without a voice I cannot say
let there be—

but in the beginning was the water.   *Min 1:01 Water*
from the water comes all that speaks.

we always want back to the water
can't you hear it roaring behind you?

keep turning, metallic eternity thing   *Min 1:21 abstract cuts*
become a wave on the Bohemian shore   *with turning movement*

roll across the Saxon steppes full
of meadows, pine trees, stones in the track bed.

later the loose piles of gravel, but still
the same soft sand underneath us.

we were born of the water
in trains we came rolling back.

later still we were children   *Min 4:57 Town-hall clock*
and already no two of us alike

that you are a twin, only occurs
to you as someone else performs

the old Welcome and Farewell
in the Palace of Tears again

just look how they're acting out
the history teacher mutters

such a spectacle at Friedrichstraße!
and who is shut up here anyway

us or them? *were i but a little bird*
with my two little wings

you carry your twin in your voice box   *Min 5:48 grey sky,*
you cry out in two dialects: *metal scaffolding*

:'.:

down with you, you party spooks   *Min 6:49 Shop-window*
disappearing into the underground station   *mannequins*

what's that tumbling across the street   *Min 6:59 blowing paper*
time travellers between the years?

swarms of weary tourists?
ghostly apparition in black-and-white   *Min 7:27 black-and-white cat*
films that no one knows anyway?

keep up, you Madonna-runners   *Min 07:38 tired passers-by*
eyes front past the explosion of colours   *overacting*
past the giantesses on the posters   *bizarre luggage*
    past the Litfaßsäule
my girl. i fly to you   *Min 7:50 pigeons*
because it can be so!

once again an epoch   *Min 8:28 train leaves the station*
takes its mechanical course.

up you go, you half-broken shutters! out with you, eiderdowns and children! there was once a parallel dimension, where millions of children were never driven to school. we went on foot! and that is us still walking, for all of this, all of this, is happening at the same time, even if you cannot hear a sound. time is Edmund Meisel's vanished music, or put the other way round: time is Edmund Meisel's piano composition that is still played today.

Min 15:40 shutters open

:',:

up you go, you broken-down shutters! let's get a look at the horses of our favourite cousin's neighbour! he's been driving a limo for years, and bids good morning to everyone. it's true that if you don't graft you're stuck here for ever, where the centuries slumber in the Gleisdreieck Park, rabbits wallowing in them. so keep turning little Lene, metallic girl, turn the tiny key, wind up the clockwork, here's another epoch taking its mechanical course.

Min 18:00 blinds up

there is a fundamental distinction
between quality time and work

Min 22:30 typewriters

we must keep on running
and talking about work, chop-chop,

always something more to be done.
define inertia, what's that about

fun? and what is it you do?
i grind my organ in the sand.

Min 24:13 End of Act II

ACT III

Min 24:16

Min 24:22 out of the tunnel

but don't turn around
for if you laugh or turn your back

you'll end up getting quite a smack
from your own squabbling family

which is on the move, trying to flee.
bogeyman, snow-white twin!

n.b., on the outer edge of the image
also important to distinguish

between sight and oversight
like hearing and hearsay

Min 25:10 man talking to the crowd

because it makes a difference
whether you tell the singing kid

'button your lip, that's all' or
'turn your face to the wall'

Heidestraße Hauptbahnhof
isn't that someone there   *Min 26:14 men arguing*

building something new?

important to distinguish too   *Min 27:23 woman staring secretly*
between tourists and refugees   *at a black man*

the tourist as the desire for invisibility
despising all other tourists

the refugee as the diminutive form
'tell us the score. was it bad?'

don't catch a chill, dearest girl
made of German steel. the jogging

spirits perform their daily circuits
round the pillar to the left of the screen

and leave animal tracks showing where
they've been in the black-and-white snow.   *Min 28:20 car with*
                                                    bride and father

which, in the instant it lands
on the machines, begins to melt away

but don't you notice something   *Min 28:48 omnibuses*
someone, falling, falling apart
or is it only about the new here?

and did you see that gold-leaf   *Min 29:00 woman climbs*
glittering under the asphalt   *the church steps*

or was that just the German
press pack on the riverbank?

time is a twin of the world running   *Min 29:12 collapsed horse*
at full throttle, turning it on
its head, it isn't ready to be read

any longer from beginning to end
but in a . . . a . . . round. just hear it out

from the Rotes Rathaus hear the chime
of who knows what—could it be time?

at this precise moment   *Min 31:03 man in a lungi*
a horse stumbles
on the freshly laid cobbles of the street.

⁚́⁚

Arrival at Anhalter Bahnhof   *Min 31:28 train arrives into*
                               Anhalter Bahnhof station

once the cattle market took place here
later the old folk with stars were shipped off

a few third-class carriages added on
to the trains to be uncoupled again

in Theresienstadt. hitch a ride, they say here,
don't turn around! metallic girl, turn onto your

side, press your ear to the sports ground
the beat of all the trains under the studs

of the players from Türkyemspor
pssst! can you hear that too?

i have baked myself coins.

i say, let light metal be the currency   *Min 32:22 Lufthansa plane*
i use to build airports too

and you can scram, with your lousy scams
no way man, you'll not get zilch from me

goddam, and now now my card has got
stuck again in the rail station

ticket machine: these Star Wars kids   *Min 33:01 Hotel boys*
slip them as a talisman

into their siblings' cradles
which are made of kinetic sand.

turn, keep turning, metallic girl *Min 39:26 plates*
'til you're dizzy with it, ears are ringing. *turning*

stuff yourself with apples from skips, eat your fill *Min 39:36 food*
so you never have to still your hunger *waste*

with tap water again. just before the
total darkness falls i long to lose

myself to a Pokémon, ha! ha!, and this
here i bequeath to your real creatures *Min 40:00 people*
the wild boars in the allotments *on the steps,*
elephants

the pair of grey foxes in the car park

in Charlottenburg and those impossibly *Min 39:20 animals*
numerous rabbits of yours, Hasenheide *in the zoo*

once again an epoch is taking *Min 40:40 boatman*
its mechanical course

it's already flickering in your neck
of the woods. TV? not got one yet?

do you remember: remembering in *Min 41:23 mother and*
black and white: how did it go again *daughters in white dresses*

do you still know, sweet metallic child?
had i but wings i'd fly to you

Min 41:44 *children*
playing in the gutter

but now keep on turning, girl
till you're dizzy with it, ears ringing

Min 45:46 *revolving door,*
rollercoaster, spirals

my favourite cousin's neighbour
must be some kinda big shot

he tells your uncle to chauffeur him
because he has the higher rank

wind up the window
that must be the Wind of Change

Min 46:26 *wind*

watch out or it'll break, it'll break
if you keep on turning it

the favourite cousin's Rubik's cube
lies broken under the bed

Min 46:42 *woman*
attempting suicide

that must have been my twin

Min 46:50 *roaring water*

now and then, according to police statistics
people lose other people

Min 47:32 *train travels*
across the image

for no particular reason. not funny!
though Berliners keep on growing back

Min 47:46 *people*
after the storm

under the radio tower buses unload
fans of all age groups

no shots again today, no explosions
instead real golden ducats, two

handfuls of sand in both pockets.
we hurry into the flickering chaos   *Min 48:43 wheels come to a stop*

we wash our hands in the sand.   *Min 48:51 factory workers washing*

⠵⠅

Min 51:07 Outing in the park

all good.
all good. thanks for asking.

twice a day. thanks for asking.
they text their Siamese sisters

boys with black eyelashes have hidden snow in the bushes

as a treat we go shopping under the rustling trees of Görlitzer Park

Min 51:54 model on the catwalk in

the evening

unmoved above it all the radio tower like mother in front of the TV-screen

as the people knocked on the roofs of the Trabis
and hugged one another on the street

and mother's twin called out
at the top of her lungs:

no, that's right!
that collective madness . . .
is realized, well, just like that!

run and buy me a ticket for Berlin
and with my own mouth i'll build you

a future made of kinetic sand.   *Min 52:41 couples sitting on benches*

ACT V   *Min 53:00*

celluloid, scissors and light   *Min 54:37 neon advertisement*

have no place in dreamers' gobs, right
or do they? spit it out, you greedy thing

and yet the little creature is still moving!
keep on turning, metallic girl   *Min 55:21 varieté dancers*

but don't turn my words inside out.   *Min 56:51 curtain falls*
shine for me instead as a sign

that even in this light cut to pieces
there's someone still there, someone speaking   *Min 57:07 people*

streaming out of the theatre

⁖,⁖

and so, for the final act, we must distinguish between thirst and hunger, desire and tongues. there was a metallic girl called Magdalene, and she first warmed herself up, then left me behind ice-cold. she peered into all the windows and installed antennae on all the radio buildings of the city, until i sobbed so long that Magdalene forgot how to look or listen. do you remember, iron Lene?

Min 57:14 couple get in, begging child stays outside

∴,∵

do you remember, Leipzig, where i called out to the oversized angel from the last ice age on its White Elster, that not even ten Pokémons, ha! ha!, would ever tempt me away from here? in the home port of Neukölln they are playing a church-asylum case and i have such a thirst for apples. eat your fruits of light metal. we won't flee anywhere at all. we will shoot oursleves snow-white into space.

Min 58:00 ice-skaters turning circles

Min 58:17 skiers

∴,∵

turn, keep on turning, you light
turn your circles. shine out white, white

forget all the creatures in the dark
forget all the colours of human skin

Min 59:43 wet street
Min 59:53 welding work at night

keep turning without sound or emotion
keep turning for ever, circling round   *Min 1:00:26 drunk man*
                                                            holding forth

tomorrow a new epoch
will take its mechanical course

so that your own rebellious tone
the tone of the story-telling beast

will be strange to you. shine hard   *Min 1:02:00 Double-decker bus*
dot dot dot, dash dash dash, dot dot dot   *from behind*

dot dot dot. travel hopefully   *Min 1:02:10 wet, image of night*
dash dash dash. travel by glittering   *traffic begins to turn*

night, dot dot dot.   *Min 1:02:18 fireworks, radio tower*

94

dot dot dash dash dash dot dot dot dot dot dash

CLOSING CREDITS

Zippelonika

This cycle deals with motherhood depression and alcoholism, and is a commission for the cellist and director Ulrike Ruf. The premiere set by Iris ter Schiphorst and sung by the Berlin Girls' Choir took place in July 2023. The children's clapping rhyme about Zippelonika, I owe to my daughter Mathilda.

Seven Marian Songs with Hyena

This little song-cycle with a hyena as a power animal was set to music by Dariya Maminova for speakers, baritone and piano. Together we performed at the premiere on 17 October 2017 in the Hochschule für Musik und Tanz in Cologne.

The Silent Songs of the Walls

As a child I used to enjoy playing in the overgrown rose garden belonging to the Castle of Tiefenau in Saxony, though the castle itself had already been blown up in 1948. As a teenager, I would draw the fountain sculptures with their decaying sandstone and during summer storms I would hide in the cavalier houses.

The land reform of October 1945 had already led to looting of the palaces and castles in the entire eastern zone. Insofar as it had not already been destroyed or plundered by the troops of the Soviet-occupying power (or local residents) in the last days of the war and the weeks afterwards, all remaining mobile inventory was taken to the Albertinum Museum in Dresden over the next few months and sold from there. The baroque castle was home to a strikingly beautiful double-barrelled staircase. The news magazine *Die Zeit* reported in 1949: 'By the time the State Monuments Office decreed, in the midst of all the destruction, that at least the statues adorning the staircase should be recovered, they had already been smashed to pieces and lay in ruins.'

Today the rose garden is being restored, the baroque castle will be rebuilt and become the centre of a golf resort. The baroque chapel in the immediate vicinity, built in 1716–17 by Elisabeth Friederike Pflug, was restored in the nineties. In keeping with the love of symmetry in the High Baroque, it has an organ dummy in the gallery on the right, which mirrors the real Silbermann organ on the left-hand side. In 2018, I laid out posters printed with the 'Silent Songs of the Walls' on thermal blankets in the sanctuary of the chapel, weighed down with rubble from the former castle, where they remained for six months for visitors to read.

Fire Earth Water Leap

The four poetic variations are based on extracts and ideas from the autobiographical novel *Der Überläufer* (The Deserter) by Wilhelm Lehmann (1882–1968), best known as a nature poet. Written in 1927 and published only in excerpts in the early sixties, it is now considered one of the most radical anti-war novels in the German language. This wide-ranging text explores the war that marks the end of German colonial history. Hanswilli Nuch, a sensitive middle-aged academic, is called up in the closing year of the war and encounters the brutality of the military. Trying to escape its bogus solidarity and toxic hierarchies, Nuch risks his life by deserting; his 'leap' out of the trench finally allowing him to cross over to the British Army. In the poems, extracts from the novel are spoken by Bruce, named after an automatic speech software. The piece also includes quotations from Lehmann's 1957 radio essay 'Gespräch über Bäume' (A Conversation About Trees). Sandig produced *Fire Earth Water Leap* in 2018 together with her sound-cosmonaut Sebastian Reuter as a short radio play.

Rhapsody of Losing

This carpet is for my daughter Mathilda. It refers to an early poem by Wilhelm Lehmann, better known under its later title, 'An meinen ältesten Sohn' (To My Eldest Son). In a later version of Lehmann's novel *Der Überläufer* (The Deserter), the poem is spoken by the protagonist, Nuch, at a piano recital.

The full text of Lehmann's poem rendered into English by the translator of this volume is as follows:

> The wintersweet the summersweet
> Bloom apart—
> In the time between, my son,
> All the world is quiet.
>
> The swallow-wort draws chalk from the cliff
> With white teeth.
> Through the dark I see it
> Dark beneath.
>
> On greying stones the raindrops run –
> The final note
> Catches in the yellowhammer's throat:
> You sing it, my son.

Murmurations. Small Choral Piece with Braces

This concrete poem is a commission for the composer and overtone singer Jan Heinke. The premiere of *Starlings*, his choral piece based on it, was held in Autumn 2020 in the Dresden Annenkirche, and sung by the Jungen Ensemble Dresden.

Guidance on Laughing at a Distance

In spring 2020 Christian Hippe, from the Literaturforum im Brecht-Haus in Berlin, invited me to write a blog on social distancing, a novel concept during the first lockdown. Grigory Semenchuk and I set the poem to music for Jens Burde's 'Museum of Slowness', a walk-through installation made of paper and moving pictures, at the Literaturhaus in Freiburg in June 2020.

When the theatre black-out and other pandemic-related restrictions continued into the following year, we decided to turn our musical rendition into a film. Sascha Conrad's poetry-film of the same name works with a paper-art set made by Estefania Conrad exclusively for this project. The film can be viewed at several international film and literature festivals, as well as on my YouTube channel: https://bit.ly/45J6Cb9 (all weblinks last accessed on 24 August 2023).

The tongue is a needle. And I am True North. Telling lies.

The title is a line from the poem 'Magnetic' by Emma McGordon, a British spoken-word poet from Cumbria. The poem deals with her (linguistic) heritage in the west of Cumbria.

Several endangered species of sea turtles lay their eggs on the beaches of the Gili-Isles, the three low-lying islands off the coast of Indonesia, threatened by global warming and rising sea levels.

Open Arms

The poem is dedicated to the crews of the rescue ships off the Italian coast.

Internal report of a Russian spy software on the up-to-the-minute state of its unsuspecting informant, codename: Cents (leaked)

The German original of the third strophe is an anagram based on the phrase 'An end to Belgium is not in sight', which appears in historian Christoph Driessen's *Gesichchte Belgiens* (History of Belgium, 2018).

we were here

This balloon poem was set to music with the poetry collective Landschaft and made into a film. The text of the poem reads as follows:

> come on / i'll build us a house / made of propane gas and flame / are you one of those / lousy fathers out to screw with my mind with that iron will of / yours, 'cos men are mechanics after all? / am i one of those miserable moms / playing dumb with their kids, leaking their feelings all over the shop? come on. // we lay in the waving grass turning

over those damned silver leaves one by one. but / were always one short. is there enough to paint the walls? is there the stuff for us / to have it all: the house with silver forks a golden retriever? / you and me / we are / so done with these old family homes. / i am the kid with the aviator goggles and you / my Hans with breadcrumbs in his head. / man / i want more than to read the coffee / grounds of chromosomes and that in the past tense! / so you take / your retriever and me my norm / we'll leave nothing here. / oh / above the ruffled fur-formation of this golden summer land- / scape a balloon rises into the sea of air. / okay / let's say a / single pinch of pathos as ballast. no more on board! // *in a forest dell there lies a house / ruined since / the woodman's death. / there 'neath the vines / and boughs, i oft-times go to seek my rest.* / fir- / cones above us, cornflowers, poppies / candles in all the trees / a party! // a balloon can sink / just think. / a balloon can't be steered. so / write it into the warmer air: // **we were here**. / you were propane / & i your flame.

 Scan the QR code to view the poetry-film on YouTube

bittersweet Ode-zine 2 (J)

The title is an anagram of 'Jetzt toben sie wieder', a work of art by the artist Daniel Rode. Since one first has to learn to say no (Nein) before one can say yes (Ja), I created the preceding free-form poem to accompany it.

Sido is a German rapper and music producer.

Friedrich Hölderlin, reworked

The lines in italics are taken from Friedrich Hölderlin's unfinished hymn 'Wie wenn am Feiertage' (As When on Holidays, 1800). Hölderlin, whose psychological disturbance was likely treated with the brutal methods of the time, spent the last three decades of his life in isolation in a tower room as the tenant of a carpenter. This poem incorporates my own lines and ideas into Hölderlin's text and is meant as a lullaby for the sleepless, the abandoned and those disappointed by the great ideologies of our own century.

Sascha Conrad's poetry-film *Leuchtende Schafe* (Shining Sheep) is available on YouTube: https://bit.ly/3sli2DL

The film is also featured in the permanent exhibition at the Hölderlin Tower in Tübingen.

Daniel dreaming

There are approx. 372 calories (kcal) in a bowl of Kellog's cornflakes. The pun on cornflakes in the original German is replaced here with Kellog's Frosties (346 kcal).

Lamentations in VI Rounds

A few years ago, I managed to leave my bank card (yet again) in a ticket machine on the Berlin underground. A young man from Afghanistan got in touch via Facebook saying he had found it. Since then, I have remained in touch with him and his large family, who live in Berlin as failed asylum seekers. The stories I was told by them formed the basis of 'Five Lamentations' which I completed some time ago.

After the Taliban took control of Kabul in August 2021, I added a sixth poem that deals with a translator left behind after the mass evacuation.

هرورو (worôra)—Oh Brother! in Pashto; بابه جان (bāba jān)—Dear Father in both Pashto and Dari.

The Songs of the Radio Tower

In the summer of 2016, I wrote a long poem inspired by Walter Ruttmann's experimental documentary film *Berlin: Die Sinfonie der Großstadt* (1927). The chronology and editing of the poem were shaped by the film's scenes and five-act structure. The star-shaped poem (see pp. 2–3 in this volume) stands at the start of it.

Modelling my writing on Ruttmann's radical editing technique, I added speech-acts from the subsequent decades without which, to my mind, present-day Berlin cannot be understood: the deportation of the Jews from the Anhalter Bahnhof, for example, or the two halves of Cold War Berlin growing ever-further apart. The Ministry for State Security was located in Magdalenenstraße in Berlin Lichtenberg and appeared in a song by the East German singer-songwriter Bettina Wegner as a femme fatale: 'Magdalena was so black and had big hands. Those whom she loved, she stroked away into the walls.' I introduced the mechanical girl ('iron Lenchen') into the cycle as a reference to that song. It is a figure that may be thought of both as the German–German twin, Berlin, but also the machine addressee of the 'Sprechgesang' (recitative) of these texts.

The poem also quotes the well-known German folksong 'Der Flug der Liebe' (The Flight of Love) about the longing symbolized by the little bird. The song is included in Achim von Arnim and Clemens Brentano's anthology of folksongs, *Des Knaben Wunderhorn* (1806).

The Friedrichstrasse 'Tränenpalast', Palace of Tears, was the check-in hall for those permitted to travel from the GDR over the border to the West.

'To hitch-hike' in German is 'per Anhalter fahren'—echoing the name of the train station.

The poem also riffs on the cautionary rhyme for children that warns about four things that do not belong in children's hands: 'Messer, Gabel, Schere, Licht' (knife, fork, scissors, matches).

'Türkiyemspor Berlin' is a Turkish association football club based in Berlin.

The poet and rapper Grigory Semenchuk (from Lviv in Ukraine) brought my poems and Walter Ruttmann's film together in an loop-based electronic composition. At the same time, this soundtrack allows for a great deal of improvisation in concert. The vocals are not fixed, many of the electronic sounds and melodies can be varied or added live such that it can sound different with each performance. A live audio recording of one of our performances of the film music accompanying Walter Ruttmann's legendary film is available online at: https://bit.ly/45IumME.

SHINING THANKS

To Ulrike Ruf for the production of 'Zippelonika'; to the Künstlerhaus Villa Concordia in Bamberg for supporting the 'Marian Songs'; Heiner Sandig for help researching the 'Silent Songs of the Walls'; Jan Heinke for setting the 'Murmurations'; Michael Augustin for the 'Conversation about Trees'; to the Wilhelm-Lehmann-Gesellschaft for the inspiration for 'Fire Earth Water Leap'; to Daniel Rode for his works 'Jetzt toben sie wieder' and 'Daniel, so nachdenklich'; the Burg Hülshoff Literature Centre for commissioning 'we were here' for the Poetry Path; to the Sarwari family for their stories of Afghan refugees; Estefania Conrad for the paper-art; Sascha Conrad for the films; Grigory Semenchuk for the music; indeed, to all the supporters of the poetry collective Landschaft for their shared enthusiasm; to Sebastian Reuter for the sound; and to our daughter Mathilda for 'Zippelonika' and the title of this book.

TRANSLATOR'S ACKNOWLEDGEMENTS

The translator is grateful to those editors who have published poems from this collection, or early versions of them, and to the journals, books and projects in which they have appeared: 'And Other Poems', *Circumference*, *Cross Language Infections*, *Fieldnotes*, *Modern Poetry in Translation*, *PNR*, *Poetry London*, *Shearsman* and *The Faust Shop*. 'Rhapsody of Losing' was commissioned for the Hay Festival 2018 and appeared in *The Echoes Last So Long: Commemorating the Armistice* (Hay Festival Press, 2018); 'Question' and 'Bittersweet Ode-zine (J)' appeared in *Daniel Rode, Again and Again* (Berlin: Hatje Cantz, 2022). The English-language film version of *Shining Sheep* was longlisted for the Brush & Lyre Prize (Palette Poetry); shortlisted for Empres Award; and selected for the Nature & Culture International Poetry Film Festival in Copenhagen in November 2021; the 'Zippelonika' cycle was selected for Versopolis 2022.

Some of the poems from this collection appeared in the pamphlet, --- – – – ---, for Ledbury Poetry Festival (Hereford: Five Seasons Press, 2023)

LIST OF POEMS

Zippelonika

O	awake	7
Z	how to wake her loser mama	8
I	the problem is	10
P	grown	11
P	on good days Zippelonika is a bouncy castle . . .	12
E	because	13
L	Zippelonika	14
O	Pixi	15
N	Chorale	16
I	why is everything starting to sway	17
K	Drinking Song	18
A	Question	19

Seven Marian Songs with Hyena

VII	Kapuzinerberg	23
VI	of Hélène	24
V	song for two voices	25
IV	over your little face	26
III	maws	27
II	look here!	28
I	echo	29

The Silent Songs of the Walls

I	33
II	34
III	35

Fire Earth Water Leap

I	Fire	39
II	Earth	41
III	Water	43
IV	Leap	44
	Rhapsody of Losing	46

Shining Bodies

Murmurations. Little Choral Piece with Braces	51
Guidance on Laughing at a Distance	52
Climate change is here, now . . .	54
from the water	56
Of Losing	57
The tongue is a needle. And I am True North. Telling lies.	58
Open Arms	59
Internal report of a Russian spy software . . .	60
saʊnd bɒdiz	62
we were here	63
bittersweet ode-zine 1 (N)	64
bittersweet ode-zine 2 (J)	65
Friedrich Hölderlin, reworked	66
Daniel dreaming	68

Lamentations in VI Rounds

round I	73
round II	74
round III	75
round IV	76
round V	78
round VI	78

The Songs of the Radio Tower

Act I	81
Act II	83
Act III	84
Act IV	88
Act V	93

Closing Credits   97
Shining Thanks   104
Translator's Acknowledgements   105